Just Call Me Daddy

The Impact of the Father–Daughter Relationship

by

Dr. Shanta McClurkin Joyner

© 2025 · Dr. Shanta McClurkin Joyner

Published by Dr. Shanta McClurkin Joyner

Table of Contents

Dedications 4

Preface 8

Introduction 10

Prologue 18

THE GOOD ONES 21

The Good Ones 23

THE COMPLICATED 47

The Complicated 49

THE UNSPOKEN 77

The Unspoken… 79

Epilogue 100

Resource Guide 102

Final Thought 106

Appendix 107

Informed Consent 108

Survey Questions & Answer Choices 108

Acknowledgments 118

About the Author 120

Dedications

To my daddy, Jesse James McClurkin, Jr.

Daddy's girl, always. That's who I was, that's who I am, and that's who I will always be.

I know now what I didn't fully realize then: not every daughter had what I had. My story is rare. While so many women carry the ache of absent or fractured fatherhood, I was blessed with a dad who showed up. Every single day. Whether you were in uniform heading off to serve or at home making us a tasty meal, I always knew I was safe, seen, and loved.

Home was wherever you were. You didn't have to raise your voice to be strong; your strength was steady, certain, and quiet. In your discipline, in your hugs, in the way you looked at me like I mattered, I found a foundation that has carried me all my life.

I didn't always understand the depth of that foundation. To me, being loved that well was normal. Watching you love on momma was natural. Only later, listening to other daughters' stories, did I realize what a gift I had been given. Confidence. Safety. The ability to believe I was worthy of love. All of that came from you.

And even when I stumbled or made choices I regret, I know it wasn't because you failed me. You gave me the tools. You gave me love. You gave me you.

Daddy, I love you. Always. That love doesn't need paragraphs or explanations. It just is. Deep, unconditional, and lifelong. I carry you with me in every strong step I take, in every decision where I choose to rise, to heal, and to love better.

You are everything a father should be. Pretty close to perfect in my eyes. And for that, I will forever be grateful.

Love always,
Chudney Shanta

To Laura Irvin —

Your story, *"Between Two Names: A Daughter's Journey Toward Peace,"* touched the heart of this book long before it was finished. You gave voice to the complex truth of living between two father figures — one absent, one present but imperfect — and the space that exists when love is both given and withheld.

I will always remember the excitement in your voice when I first told you this book would be published. The joy and pride you carried in that moment are stitched into these pages, a reminder that this work is not mine alone but also yours.

You showed us what it means to carry gratitude and grief at the same time; to navigate the ache of longing alongside the strength of survival. Your courage to share your journey, your resilience in the face of broken bonds, and your search for peace are a gift to every daughter who has ever felt incomplete.

Though you are no longer here to hold this book in your hands, your spirit lives in every word. You remind us that the story of a daughter is never simple, never one-sided, but always filled with hope, healing, and the power to grow.

This book is dedicated to you, Laura; a daughter who teaches us all what it means to find peace between two names. Forever remembered and loved.

Laura F. Irvin

10/23/1971 - 11/30/2021

"Some fathers build daughters with love; others teach them how to rebuild themselves."

— Dr. Shanta McClurkin Joyner

Preface

For years, I couldn't understand why I couldn't seem to get relationships right. On paper, I had everything that should have made love easy — an amazing father who showed me what protection, care, and consistency looked like. My daddy was my hero. He was kind, patient, and present. I never doubted his love for me, and I thought that would automatically translate into healthy romantic relationships.

But it didn't.

After two divorces and countless broken relationships, I started to question myself. How could someone who grew up with such a solid example of love still find herself lost in love? The more I reflected, the more I realized that my father's love had actually set a high standard—one that I refused to lower. His example taught me what love was supposed to look and feel like, which meant I couldn't stay where peace was absent or where respect was negotiable.

Now, in this season of my life, I am remarried — and it feels like home. It's full of the green flags I prayed for: peace, safety, laughter, and partnership. I finally understand that all those "failed" relationships weren't really failures. They were lessons preparing me to recognize the kind of love my father modeled — steady, kind, and rooted in mutual respect.

This book grew from my personal reflection into a deeper research journey. I wanted to understand the psychology behind the father–daughter bond and its lifelong impact. I needed to know why that connection shapes how we love, trust, and choose. Through that exploration, I found not just answers, but purpose.

I began writing this book in 2019, inspired by the voices and experiences of women who, like me, had stories tied to their fathers. I created survey questions for these women to answer and later converted their responses into narrative form. This was a huge task, and I did not take it lightly — trying to express their feelings, their stories, and their experiences in my words while staying true to their voices.

After collecting their heartfelt responses, I came to a halt— emotionally full, unsure how to move forward with all that truth. During that hiatus, one of the women who shared her story passed away. That loss was another sign that I MUST publish this book — to honor her story and the stories of the others who trusted me with their truth.

In 2025, I decided that I would finish what I started. I am releasing this book on my father's 75th birthday, November 4, 2025. Jesse James McClurkin, Jr., this is for you.

Just Call Me Daddy isn't just about my story — it's about becoming the standard, not the statistic. It's about recognizing that love isn't about perfection; it's about presence, growth, and grace. My hope is that these pages help other daughters understand their reflections, rebuild where necessary, and celebrate the men who showed them how to expect nothing less than real love.

Introduction

Just Call Me Daddy

There is a space in every woman's life. A quiet, pulsing corner of her heart that carries the imprint of her father.

For some, it's a full-color memory: his laugh echoing down hallways, his arms a shelter from the world, his wisdom shaping her steps. For others, it's a vacant chair at the dinner table, a phone call that never came, a door that closed and never reopened.

This book is for all of them.

For the women who never knew the sound of their father's voice
but hear his absence in every room they enter.
For the ones raised by strong men who stepped in; grandfathers,
uncles, stepfathers, trying to patch the hole a biological father left
behind.
For the women who had amazing fathers, who kissed scraped knees
and danced at every recital, yet somehow still found themselves
drawn to the wrong men, chasing love in all the wrong places.
For the women who had great fathers and great homes, but still felt a
quiet ache, the kind no one talks about because everything on the
outside looked perfect. The daughters who loved and were loved by
their dads, yet battled insecurities, questions, and wounds they
couldn't trace. This is for them too...because a father's presence
doesn't always guarantee clarity, and sometimes, even in love,
things get lost.
For the daughters of addicts, of abusers, of men whose own
wounds spilled onto the ones they were supposed to protect.
And for the daughters of kind, quiet men who stayed physically,
but left emotionally.

"Daddy issues," they call it, as if it were a punchline. A stereotype
wrapped in shame.
But here, we're unwrapping it.

We're peeling back the layers and sitting in the truth of it all: that the
father-daughter bond, whether full, fractured, or nonexistent, has
the power to shape the woman she becomes. That no matter how
strong a mother is, or how brave a daughter tries to be, the
presence, or absence, of a father ripples into everything: our sense of
safety, our idea of love, our worth, our voice, our choices.

We've heard the research. The statistics. The studies that say girls without fathers are more likely to live in poverty, drop out of school, or end up in toxic relationships.
But what about the girls who didn't? The ones who broke the mold?
And just as importantly, what about the ones who didn't have to? Who had fathers at home, doing everything "right," yet still felt something missing?

This book is not about blame.
It is not about pity.
It is about truth.

Real women. Real stories. Raw, vulnerable, and complex. From daughters of all races, faiths, and families. From different zip codes, income levels, and beliefs. They've offered up their stories—some stitched with pain, others with healing. All with courage.

Because sometimes a father is a hero.
Sometimes, he's a heartbreak.
And sometimes… he's just not there.

But every woman in these pages has found her voice. Some are still searching. Some have forgiven. Some are still grieving. Some are just beginning to understand how much of their journey started with a man called *Daddy*.

Whatever your story, you are not alone.

This is for the women who've whispered questions into pillows at night, wondering, *Why didn't he stay? Why didn't he see me? Why wasn't I enough?*
This is for the women who've built lives with bricks made from silence, from strength, from survival.
And it's for the fathers, too! Those who tried, those who failed, those who left, and those who loved as best they could.

In these stories, you'll find pain. But also resilience. Reflection. And sometimes… redemption.

When Love Doesn't Add Up: The Myth of the Guarantee

There's a comforting assumption we like to believe: if a girl has a good father, she will grow up to make good choices in love. It's a tidy equation, easy to understand and repeat. But real life isn't math. And love, especially the kind we seek in adulthood, isn't always logical.

The truth is far more complicated. The father-daughter relationship is one of the most emotionally formative bonds in a girl's life, and researchers have long documented its impact on her psychological development. Dr. Linda Nielsen, professor of adolescent and educational psychology at Wake Forest University, found that daughters with warm, supportive fathers tend to have higher self-esteem, do better in school, and form healthier romantic relationships later in life. Yet even the most loving father cannot fully protect his daughter from heartbreak, and the absence of one doesn't doom her to it either.

When Good Dads Can't Prevent Bad Choices

Take Melanie. She grew up with a devoted father who never missed a recital and constantly reminded her of her worth. Yet at 28, she found herself leaving a third toxic relationship in five years. "I had a great dad," she said. "So why was I settling for men who made me feel small?"

Through therapy, she realized she wasn't seeking love, she was seeking validation. Somewhere along the way, her father's praise had transformed into a belief that she needed a man's approval to feel worthy. When that adoration was withheld, she chased it harder, even when it hurt.

Jasmine's story echoes this truth. Her father was her hero; loving, consistent, and proud. Yet she married a man who belittled and isolated her. "I thought I could love him enough to make him better," she confessed. Love, she learned, isn't supposed to hurt— and even good fathers can't insulate daughters from cultural messages, peer pressure, or hidden wounds that distort what love looks like.

When Absent Fathers Don't Define the Future

Janessa's father disappeared when she was six. For years, she built walls around her heart, convinced she didn't need anyone. It wasn't until she met Marcus, patient, kind, and emotionally steady, that she recognized she was punishing him for wounds he didn't cause.
Healing took time, therapy, and faith. "My marriage became my greatest act of trust," she now says.

Daniella's father also left early. Raised by her single mother, she turned her pain into purpose, becoming a therapist who helps others heal relationship trauma. "I built my relationship like a house with a blueprint," she said. "Deliberate and thoughtful. I didn't want chaos, so I studied peace."

These women prove that fatherlessness isn't a life sentence. As one *Child Development* study revealed, some daughters who experienced abandonment or neglect developed stronger emotional resilience, becoming more discerning in love. Pain, when faced honestly, can become wisdom.

What the Research Shows

A 2015 *Journal of Family Psychology* study found that the **quality**, not just the **presence**, of the father-daughter relationship predicted how daughters approached intimacy and boundaries. Daughters of emotionally available fathers tended to communicate needs clearly and set limits. Those with distant or unpredictable fathers often experienced anxiety in love—oscillating between neediness and withdrawal.

Dr. Jennifer Freyd's research on betrayal trauma adds another layer: even daughters of loving fathers can carry hidden wounds from emotional neglect or lack of attunement—wounds that quietly shape how they love and what they tolerate.

And as Dr. Linda Nielsen reminds us, "The father's influence on his daughter's romantic life is significant, but not predictive in a vacuum. Environment, personal resilience, support systems, and her internal narrative matter just as much."

The Internal Narrative

What does a woman believe about herself, and what she deserves? That story often determines the relationships she chooses.

If a girl grows up believing she is unlovable, she may seek partners who confirm that lie. But if she surrounds herself with truth-tellers; mentors, friends, teachers, therapists, her story can change.

Conversely, even girls with stable fathers can falter if they were never taught to recognize red flags or advocate for their own needs. Love without wisdom is not protection.

Beyond the Script

Relationships often mirror what we learned, or didn't learn, about love at home. Some women repeat patterns. Some rebel against them. Some rebuild entirely.

Carmen watched her mother chase unavailable men and vowed never to depend on one. She married late, to a man who respected her independence. Lauren grew up in a picture-perfect home and mistook endurance for love. "I thought staying, no matter what, meant loyalty," she said. "Now I know the difference between commitment and self-sacrifice."

Writing a New Ending

The myth that a "good dad" guarantees a "good life" is comforting but incomplete. What shapes a woman's future is not just her father's presence or absence, but her interpretation of the experience—the healing she chooses, the truths she embraces, and the boundaries she builds.

Because fatherlessness is not a curse.
 And father presence is not a perfect shield.

In the end, who a girl becomes depends on more than the love she received—it's shaped by how she learns to love herself.

Prologue

The Weight and Wonder of the Word "Daddy"

"Daddy."
The word comes out like breath in the mouths of little girls; soft, sweet, full of trust. It's one of the first titles of love we learn to speak.

And for many, it remains a name wrapped in safety. A source of laughter, of unwavering presence, of wisdom offered without judgment. There are daughters who danced on their daddy's shoes, who felt seen every day of their lives, who never had to question whether they were cherished. This book celebrates them too—
those whose fathers didn't just show up, but showed *how* to love well. Men who were steady. Gentle. Present. Who helped their daughters build confidence and boundaries and a belief in their own worth.

But not every daughter had that gift.

For some, "Daddy" was a name attached to pain. To silence. To shadows that stretched across childhood and spilled into womanhood. There are daughters who learned early that the man in the house could also be the one who made them feel small. Who stole their innocence. Who broke their spirit with words, or worse. Daughters who were left bruised—not just on the body, but on the soul.

Some fathers vanish. Some destroy.
And some... stay, but never actually see you.

This book holds all of it.

The light and the dark. The beautiful and the brutal. The love that built, and the absence that broke. Because no two daughters carry the same story—and yet, the imprint of a father touches everything: our sense of self, our ability to trust, how we receive love, and how we give it.

Here, we honor the complexity.

We celebrate the fathers who got it right.
We mourn the ones who couldn't—or wouldn't.
And we hold space for the women still sorting through the ashes and trying to find their way back to themselves.

Because every daughter's journey is sacred.

Some grew from rich soil. Others from cracked concrete. But all deserve to be seen. So, whether you are a woman who adored her father, feared him, lost him, or never really knew him—this book is for you.

Your story belongs here. Welcome.

This is not just a book. It's a mirror.
And in it, every woman might find a piece of herself.

So turn the page, daughter.
We're beginning.

THE GOOD ONES

"A daughter needs a dad to be the standard against which she will judge all men."
— Gregory E. Lang

The Good Ones

Not every story of a father–daughter relationship begins in pain. Some begin in peace… in homes where laughter filled the walls, where a father's voice calmed storms before they ever reached his little girl's heart. These are the men who understood the assignment early: protect her, teach her, and love her in a way that makes the world seem less cruel.

The good dads don't make headlines or become hashtags. They don't always have the loudest voices, but they leave echoes that last for generations. They show up in the small moments — sitting on bleachers in the rain, fixing broken toys, giving talks that end with "You've got this." They become the silent standard for every man who follows.

They are the blueprint; the reason some daughters know what safety feels like, what kindness looks like, and what love sounds like when it doesn't have to prove itself. These fathers raise daughters who see themselves as worthy, not because someone told them so, but because they watched it modeled every single day.

This section is a love letter to the good ones. The fathers who led with grace, patience, and presence. The men who taught their daughters to dream big, walk tall, and never apologize for expecting respect. These stories remind us that good fathers are not mythical creatures; they are steady hands and open hearts, shaping futures with quiet strength.

To the daughters who were blessed with good dads, hold on to those memories and keep telling those stories. To the men who *are* those dads, know that your love ripples far beyond your home. You are the proof that good men still exist. You are the reminder that fatherhood, when done with heart, changes everything.

When Love Was Real – The Daughters Who Were Seen
Anonymous

Not every story begins in pain.

Some of us were raised by men who were safe places, solid ground, steady arms. Men who came home when they said they would. Who knelt to tie little shoes and stood to cheer at big games. Who asked questions and actually listened. Who told us we were beautiful *before* anyone else did, and not just for how we looked— but for how we thought, how we dreamed, how we cared.

My dad was that man.

He wasn't perfect, but he was present. Emotionally, physically, spiritually. When I fell, he picked me up. When I doubted myself, he reminded me who I was. When the world was too loud, his voice calmed the storm inside me.

He never made me feel like too much. Or not enough. He just… loved me.

And still—*still*—I found myself in rooms with people who did not.

I dated men who dimmed my light. I questioned my worth. I compared myself. I second-guessed the same confidence my father tried so hard to instill in me.

Because even with a good dad, life happens. Culture whispers. Insecurities creep in. And being raised in love doesn't always mean we grow up immune to pain.

But having him—having that blueprint—*changed everything.*

When I finally walked away from the wrong love, I had a frame of reference. I knew what real love looked like. What patience sounded like. What accountability felt like. I had seen it in action— in the way my father spoke to my mother, in the way he prayed for us, in the way he showed up again and again and again.

That love became my compass.

So, this section is for daughters like me. The ones who grew up held. The ones who had Saturday pancakes, grits and bacon and long drives and inside jokes with the man who tucked them in every night. The ones who never had to doubt whether they were wanted. Who had love on tap, laughter in the living room, and wisdom at the kitchen table.

It's for the daughters who still cry in secret sometimes, because even in good homes, the world outside can bruise you.

It's for the women who carry a quiet guilt—like maybe they shouldn't hurt or struggle or question anything because they had such a "good" dad. Let this be your permission to feel it all. Gratitude *and* grief. Joy *and* confusion. Love *and* longing. Because having a great father doesn't mean your story is simple. It means you had a powerful start—but you're still writing the rest.

And if your father is still here, hug him harder. Call him today. Tell him thank you—not for being perfect, but for being *present*. For loving in a world that often teaches men to disappear. For showing up in ways that some daughters only dream about.

If your father is gone, remember his love was a gift, not a guarantee. Carry it proudly. Let it bloom in how you love your own children. Let it echo in how you walk through the world.

Because every time someone says, "You remind me of your dad," you get to smile and say, *"Thank you."*

This is for the daughters who were believed, who were cherished, who were seen.

You are proof that good fathers exist.

And we celebrate them, too.

The Ache with No Name
Morgan Elise

I had a great dad.

There, I said it. I need you to hear that first because so many stories start with what a father wasn't. Mine was there. Present. Protective. Gentle, even. He showed up to school plays, taught me how to ride a bike, and held my hand during my first heartbreak. He was consistent, kind, and every bit the man you'd want your daughter to look up to.

I never went hungry. Never heard him yell. Never saw him hit my mom or raise his voice in rage. We had dinner at the table every night, family vacations in the summer, and birthday cakes made from scratch.

By all accounts, I had a textbook childhood. A "you have nothing to complain about" kind of life.

And yet.

There was always… something.

Something that hummed beneath the surface, soft but persistent. A quiet ache I didn't know how to name. Like standing in a beautiful room and still feeling cold.

I didn't talk about it for years because I thought I wasn't allowed to feel it. I told myself it was ungrateful to question anything. My friends would cry over absent dads or traumatic homes, and I'd nod in sympathy, hiding the fact that I envied their clarity. Their hurt had a name. Mine was a fog.

I loved my father deeply. Still do. But love doesn't always mean full understanding. And presence doesn't always mean connection.

You see, my father was kind, but quiet. Emotionally reserved. We laughed together, worked hard, shared space—but we didn't share heart.

I never heard him say "I'm proud of you" unless it came with a certificate or a report card. We didn't talk about feelings. We didn't have long talks about life or dating or how to navigate the emotional storms of growing up as a girl in a world that always asks more. He wasn't unkind—he was just... contained. Like he was taught to love through action, not expression.

And I needed both.

As a teenager, I started feeling invisible in the very house where I was loved. Not neglected—just unseen. Like I was checking all the boxes of a good daughter, and he was checking all the boxes of a good father, but something vital kept slipping between the lines.

So I went looking for that missing piece.

And where do most girls go when they feel emotionally misunderstood by their fathers?
Boys.

At 16, I fell hard for someone who loved-bombed me with attention. At 19, I clung to a man who said everything my father never did: "You're beautiful. You matter. I see you." It didn't matter that his actions rarely matched his words—I stayed, because the words felt like water to a girl who didn't know she was thirsty.

It took me years to see the pattern: that I was chasing emotional validation in people who offered the illusion of intimacy, not the substance of it. Because even in a house full of love, I hadn't been taught how to sit with my own emotions, how to voice them, or how to ask for what I needed without guilt.

And here's the truth no one tells you:
 Sometimes, you can grow up in love and still feel lack. Sometimes, you can have a father who tried his best, and still walk away with questions.

It doesn't make you ungrateful.
 It makes you human.

I don't blame my father. I believe he did what he knew. I believe he loved me deeply in the language he was taught. But I also believe two things can be true at once:

My dad was good.
 And I still needed more.

That's a hard truth to say out loud. Because people expect trauma to come with scars and sirens. Not silence.

But this chapter is for the daughters who never got hit, never got screamed at, never got left behind, yet still struggle with feeling fully seen.

This is for the ones who look back at childhood photos and smile with their mouths but wince in their hearts.

For the women who love their fathers but wish they'd had more conversations, more vulnerability, more "I love you just because."

For the girls who were emotionally hungry in houses full of food. You're not selfish. You're not spoiled. You're not overthinking it. You are simply someone whose emotional needs weren't met in ways that matched your spirit.

And that matters too.

So here I am, learning how to love myself in the ways I needed. How to speak when I'm scared. How to sit with discomfort. How to give and receive affection without apology.

And I still talk to my dad. I still hug him when I see him. But now I know that loving him doesn't mean I have to silence my ache. Because even soft homes can leave quiet wounds. And even good fathers can have blind spots. But daughters—we keep rising anyway.

Daddy's Girl, Always
Shanta

I know that not everyone has what I have. And sometimes, when I listen to other women speak about absent fathers or strained relationships, I realize just how rare my story is. My name is Shanta, and my father, Jesse, is awesome. Simple as that.

He isn't just a father by title. He shows up. Day in and day out. Whether he was in his military uniform heading off for duty or at home making us laugh, I have always known I was safe, seen, and loved. He is present in all the ways that matter; physically, emotionally, spiritually. I feel it in his hugs, in his discipline, in the way he looks at me like I am someone who matters.

Home Was Wherever He Was
There was something powerful about knowing I could run into my father's arms and everything would be okay. That's who my daddy was for me growing up. A solid rock in a chaotic world. He didn't have to yell or demand attention. His strength was quiet. His love was
certain. Even when he didn't say much, I knew I could count on him.

I remember how he would come home from work with little treats tucked under his arm; small surprises that made me feel so special, so thought of. And I'll never forget the way he held me when my heart was broken. I cried snot and tears all over his shirt, but he didn't move. He didn't rush me or tell me to stop. He just let me fall apart until I could put myself back together again.

Our Victories Together

One of the proudest moments of my life was finishing my degree at the same time he finished his. What an accomplishment to celebrate together. We beamed with joy, not just as father and daughter, but as two people who worked hard, persevered, and reached a milestone side by side. His pride in me matched mine in him, and I will never forget that moment. We literally MASTERED it!

Strawberry Cake, Whitman's Chocolates, and Valentine Love

Every year, without fail, Daddy bakes me a strawberry cake for my birthday. It's not just cake, it's love baked into every layer, frosting smoothed with patience, joy sprinkled into every bite. Even this year, when I turned 49, he kept that tradition alive. That strawberry cake reminds me that no matter how old I get, I will always be his little girl.

And every Valentine's Day, he gives me and my sister a box of Whitman's chocolates. Always. Without fail. He is my first Valentine and my forever Valentine. Because of him, I never have to seek validation elsewhere—I already know I am loved. Maybe that's part of why some of my relationships have been broken. I knew what love was supposed to look like, and I refused to settle for less.

The Impact I Understand Now

When people ask if my relationship with my father shapes who I am, the answer is yes—absolutely. I realize now that having the steady presence of a good father changes everything: your confidence, your choices, your very sense of worth.

I've made my share of mistakes. Many. Sometimes I even shake my head and call myself "dumb me" for choices I wish I could take back. But I don't put that on him. He has always given me the tools. He has always laid the foundation. I just had to learn how to use them in my own time.

"She Can Do It"

My daddy always made me believe I could do anything. I still remember being just three or four years old, wobbling on my little bike while my mom stood nearby, worried I might fall. But Daddy just smiled proudly and said, "She can do it." And I did. Those four words have echoed through my life ever since. Whether I'm facing a new challenge, chasing a dream, or walking through hard seasons, I still hear his voice reminding me that I can do it. He taught me that nobody is better than me, but that I'm not better than anyone else, either. That balance of confidence and humility has guided me through every season of life. Now, watching him as a grandfather to my children, I see that same love and strength reflected again. In the absence of their father, he has stepped in with patience, laughter, and unwavering presence, reminding them, just as he reminded me, that they are loved, capable, and never alone.

Loving Him, Always

Daddy, I love you. That love doesn't need paragraphs or justifications. It just is. Deep, unconditional, and lifelong. I carry you with me in every strong moment. In every decision I make where I choose to rise, to heal, to love better.

You are everything a father should be. Pretty close to perfect in my eyes. And for that, I am endlessly grateful.

Forever your little girl,
Shanta

The Non-Verbal Legacy
A'Riel T.B. Winston

Some lessons in life are spoken. Others are lived. The ones that shaped me most didn't come from long conversations or heartfelt lectures, but from quiet consistency, silent sacrifice, and a steady love that didn't always need words.

My dad, D. Brown, is the truest example of what I called a *Real Man.*

A Silent Giant

Growing up, I watched my dad dedicate himself to our family in a way that left an imprint I carried into adulthood. For ten years, he commuted out of town for work, never once complaining, always providing. He was the protector, the professor, and the provider. And in one unforgettable act of selflessness, he gave up a career he had nurtured for three decades—just to keep another man from losing his job.

That is who he *still* is!

He is the kind of man whose word is his bond, whose integrity speaks volumes without needing explanation. He often told us, "Don't sweat the small stuff. All stuff *is* small stuff." And in his calm, grounded way, he has always lived that truth.

Present, Yet Distant

But even strength had its quiet shadows.

Although my dad was physically present—dependable in every way—there were moments when I needed more. Especially when it came to my relationships with men. I *wanted* his insight. I *needed* his opinions. But he rarely gave them, often deferring to me with a quiet, "Well, A'Riel, it's your life. You have to make the best decision for you."

At times, it felt as though he was emotionally absent, allowing my mother to speak on his behalf. She was the voice in our home—the one who told it like it was, whether you were ready or not. And while I appreciated her honesty, I longed to hear *my dad's* truth, his direct words, especially when I felt unsure or vulnerable.

The Long Lesson

That silence created an emotional distance between us, and it shaped how I interpreted love and value in relationships. For thirteen years, I remained in one that should have ended much sooner—waiting, perhaps, for my dad to step in and tell me what he really thought… but he never did.

Looking back, I often wondered if that was his way of teaching me something. Maybe he trusted me more than I trusted myself. Maybe his silence was a nudge toward independence. Or maybe… he just simply didn't know how to say what he felt?

And yet, despite the emotional distance, my dad gave me the best gift: *an example*. Because of him, I learned to pay attention not to a man's words, but to his actions. That's where truth lives.

The Reflection of Real

When I first wrote this reflection six years ago, I was just beginning a new chapter of my life. Jason—who had just started courting me at the time—is now my husband. We married in 2020, welcomed our first son in February of 2022, our daughter in November of 2023, and another baby boy in May of 2025.

With time, my perspective on my dad has not changed—it has deepened. I now understand his quiet strength in ways I couldn't before. Watching Jason love and lead our family with the same calm, steady presence my dad showed me growing up has brought everything full circle.

Jason shows up. He honors his word. He protects and provides in both spirit and action. It isn't just what he says—it is what he does. And maybe that was what my dad had been trying to teach me all along— not through lectures, but through a lived-out example of love, patience, and principle.

If that was the lesson… then I finally understand it.

A Daughter's Gratitude

Dad, if you ever wondered whether I saw you—I did. I *always* did.

Because of your consistency, because of your sacrifice, because of the man you were, and the man you still are, I have found a love that reflects everything you taught me to expect… without ever saying a word.

Thank you for showing me what a real man looks like.

I am, and always will be, forever grateful.

Rooted in Resilience
Anissa Alvarado

I am 41 years old today, and I know—deep down in my bones—that my father made me who I am.

Melvin Steed was born into poverty, the youngest of seven. Life didn't hand him much, but he found strength in his faith and his family. He met my mother in high school, married her soon after, and eventually served both his country and his calling—as a soldier and then as an ordained pastor. He was always steady. Always soft- spoken. Always there.

The Heart of a Father

What I remember most isn't just what he did—it's how he loved.

My father prayed for us out loud, tenderly, as if he were speaking directly into our futures. He believed in the power of words, and he used his to uplift and protect. When I was younger, I'd hear him pray for our future spouses, for their kindness and strength, for their faith and character. He believed love required vision. And he had it—for all of us.

He wasn't the kind of man who held his feelings inside. He was emotionally present, willing to cry, willing to comfort, willing to show that strength and softness could live in the same heart.

The Blueprint for Belief

Because of my dad, I grew up believing I could do *anything*. Not in a dreamy, vague kind of way—but with intention. He reminded me constantly of my goals, especially when I drifted or doubted. He celebrated my academic achievements, encouraged my growth, and reminded me of who I said I wanted to become.

I carry that voice with me even now. When life stretches me thin or tries to convince me I'm not enough, I hear him: *You've got this. You always did.*

Faith, Foundation, and Family

My father's role in my life didn't end when I became an adult—it just shifted. He's been a rock in my marriage, offering wise, steady counsel more times than I can count. Whether I'm struggling with a hard decision or just needing to be reminded that love takes work, my dad has been there—with truth, grace, and perspective.

He never disappeared. Never wavered. Never withheld love.

A Different Kind of Legacy

I know that many women live with the ache of a missing father, or the confusion of a complicated one. I don't take for granted that mine was different.

I was never a Fatherless Daughter. I was a *Father-Filled* one.

My dad's presence has taught me that love doesn't have to be loud to be lasting. That resilience is often born in quiet moments—like morning prayers or Sunday afternoon conversations. And that the truest kind of strength is the kind that nurtures.

Because of him, I am rooted. I am resilient. I am loved.

Steady Love

Jessica McClurkin Gates

When I think about my daddy, the first word that comes to mind is *steady*. His love has never been loud or showy, but it's always been there; constant, dependable, and strong. He's a man of few words, but his actions have always spoken for him. No matter what was happening or how tired he was, he showed up. Every single time.

That's just who he is. The one who made sure we were taken care of, who kept things going even when we didn't see the weight he carried. His love didn't come in long speeches or big hugs—it came in the way he worked hard, the way he paid attention, the way he made sure home was home.

Lessons in Strength and Drive

A few years ago, during a counseling session, my therapist said something that stuck with me. She told me that my constant need to plan, to move, to ask "what's next?" probably came from watching my father. At first, that hit me hard. I left that session and didn't go back because it felt like she was saying my strength was a flaw.

But looking back now, I see it differently. That drive came from watching my daddy keep going—no matter what. It came from seeing him tired but still showing up for work. From watching him make things happen even when times were tough. That kind of strength rubbed off on me.

Now, I understand that my "keep going" spirit is part of my inheritance from him. It's not about perfection—it's about perseverance.

What He Taught Me About Love

My daddy also taught me what love and marriage really look like. The way he loves my mama—with patience, humor, and quiet loyalty—set the standard for me. He never tried to be perfect, but he's always been consistent.

I'll never forget the first time I had a real disagreement with my husband. I was so upset I packed my bags and went straight to my parents' house. My mama and daddy sat me down that night and told me the truth: marriage isn't easy, and you can't run every time it gets hard. They reminded me that they had disagreements too— they just didn't have them in front of us.

That talk changed how I saw things. It reminded me that real love isn't about pretending everything's fine—it's about choosing to stay, to listen, and to keep trying. Before the night was over, they told me to go back home and work it out. And I did.

The Little Things That Stay With You

Some of my favorite memories with my daddy are the small ones. He used to do my ponytails before school, brushing my hair just right until every piece was in place. Somehow, no matter how rushed we were, he always made time to make sure I looked my best.

When it came to homework, he was my "back in the day ChatGPT." He'd make me look things up in the dictionary first, just to see if I could find it on my own. Eventually, he'd get tired of watching me struggle and just tell me the answer—but that was our thing. It wasn't really about the homework; it was about patience, about learning how to think, and about knowing he was right there beside me.

And the car rides—those are the memories that make me smile the most. He'd sneak me candy when I wasn't supposed to have any, just to make me laugh. Those moments weren't fancy or planned, but they meant the world to me.

His Mark on My Life

So much of who I am now comes from him. The way I make decisions, how I carry myself, how I handle life—it all traces back to what I saw growing up. My father taught me to think before I act, to stay calm under pressure, and to always keep moving forward.

He never sat me down and said, "This is how to live." He just lived it. By example. Through his work, his love, and his quiet strength.

Because of him, I value peace over chaos. Because of him, I understand that real love isn't loud—it's loyal. And because of him, I've learned that showing up for people, day after day, is one of the truest forms of love there is.

Reflection
My daddy gave me the kind of love that doesn't always make noise but never fades. It's in the way I love my family, the way I show up for others, and the way I carry myself through every season of life. His love is the rhythm behind my strength—the part of me that keeps going, no matter what.

A Father Who Stood Tall
Kamela Hill

The Foundation of Our Home

When I think about my childhood, one truth rises above everything else: my father believed that a man should always take care of his family—no matter how hard it was. And he lived that truth every single day.

My parents were together, always. There was never a moment of fractured loyalty, never a split household to navigate. My father was not a man who made excuses, nor was he the kind of father who disappeared when things got tough. He stayed. He worked. He prayed. And he raised us with his whole heart.

Growing Up With Presence

I was blessed to grow up in a home where my father was both physically and emotionally present. During my adolescent years— those years where so many girls feel unseen—my father made sure I knew that I was valued.

He didn't just live at home—he *lived with us*. His presence wasn't just about sharing an address; it was about investing his time, his wisdom, and his love. I remember the quiet strength he carried, the way he never had to raise his voice for us to know he was serious, the way his smile could break tension and remind us we were safe.

Raising Seven Children

My father and mother raised seven children together, and all seven of us became productive, successful adults. That is no small accomplishment. It wasn't easy—raising seven children never is— but my father led with strength and consistency.

He and my mother never sugarcoated life. They told us the truth about the world, about choices, about responsibility. Both lived by Bible standards, and they taught us to do the same. Their discipline was steady, but their love was undeniable. In that mix, we learned what it meant to live with both integrity and resilience.

Lessons That Last

Even now, at 57 years old, I still turn to my father for advice— especially about teaching. He knows the value of education, of discipline, of perseverance, and his guidance steadies me. I may be an adult with decades of experience behind me, but when my father speaks, I still lean in like I did when I was a girl. His words matter, because they carry the weight of a man who has lived with honor.

Realizing What I Had

The older I get, the more I appreciate him. It's easy to take for granted the steady presence of a good father when you're young. You don't realize how rare it is. You don't notice that what feels "normal" in your home is extraordinary compared to the silence or absence that other children endure.

Now, I look back and see my father for who he is: a man who gave his children a foundation of faith, discipline, and love strong enough to stand on for a lifetime.

Still His Daughter

I know I am not perfect. I am still working on my own imperfections, still striving to be better each day. But I know this: I had the privilege of being raised by a father who showed up, who stood tall, and who never stopped taking care of us.

Because of him, I know what it means to be steady. Because of him, I know the power of truth. And because of him, I walk through this life confident that I was, and always will be, my father's daughter.

THE COMPLICATED

"She made broken look beautiful, and strong look invincible. She walked with the universe on her shoulders and made it look like a pair of wings."
— *Ariana Dancu*

The Complicated

"Upside Down He's Turning Me" ... The Stories of Flawed Foundations

Before she knew how to spell *abandonment,* she felt it.
Before she could form sentences, she had already learned silence.
Before she understood what a father should be, she learned what it
meant when he wasn't.

This book was born from that space—the quiet ache between what
was and what should have been. It is a love letter to the daughters
who have carried the weight of father wounds in all their forms: the
loud kind, the quiet kind, the invisible ones that still shape how they
walk into rooms, how they trust, how they love.

Not every story fits neatly into "good" or "bad." Some live in the
in-between—the complicated places where love existed, but so did
confusion, silence, and unmet needs. These are the fathers who
tried but didn't always get it right. The ones who showed up in body
but not always in spirit. The ones who wanted to love deeply but were
still learning how.

Some of the women in these pages had no father at all—just a name
on a birth certificate or a photo in a drawer. Others had fathers who
lived in the same house but never looked them in the eyes. Still
others had dads who showed up to every game, every recital, every
milestone—and somehow, something was still missing.

These daughters carry both gratitude and grief in the same breath. Their
stories are not about blame, but about understanding—the kind that
only comes with time, distance, and healing. Because sometimes love
isn't absent—it's just unfinished.

This book does not live in bitterness. It lives in truth.
And truth is not always loud. Sometimes it whispers through clenched teeth. Sometimes it hums through generations.

You will meet women who are still healing. Women who have forgiven. Women who ran. Women who stayed. Women who are doing the hard, holy work of parenting their own children differently. You will meet women whose fathers gave them nightmares, and others whose fathers gave them memories—and still, the ache remained.

This is for the daughter who flinched at the sound of her name.
The one who sat by the phone, praying it would ring.
The one who defended him, even after he disappeared. The one who still asks, *"Was it me?"*
The one who wonders why her heart breaks at Father's Day cards.

This is for the woman who is thriving now—but still hears his voice when she doubts herself.
This is for every version of her.

Her name is not shame.
Her name is not broken.
Her name is *Daughter.*

And her story begins here.

My Daddy's Laughter
Hunni

He wasn't a perfect father, but he was MY DADDY—and that meant everything.

My father, Robert, had a way of filling any space he entered. He could walk into a room and instantly own it—not with power or pride, but with laughter. He did not need to say much; his laughter spoke volumes. There was something about him - an ease, a warmth - that made you feel safe. He carried stories in his voice, warmth in his eyes, and a light that drew people toward him. He could turn an ordinary moment into a memory just by being there.

Daddy wasn't without flaws—but love always found its way through the cracks. That's what I will forever hold on to - the laughter, the stories, and the light he carried everywhere he went. I'll always remember him, not for what he lacked, but for the joy he gave so freely and the life he lived - boldly, fully, and just as he pleased.

A Complicated Kind of Love

Growing up, my life was shaped by many hands—my maternal grandparents, my mother, and my stepfather—but my father always held a special place in my heart. His presence wasn't constant, but when he was around, the world seemed lighter. His laugh could cut through the hardest day. His smile could disarm anger. And even when I didn't have all of him, I felt his love in the ways that mattered most to a daughter—simple moments, big memories, and an unspoken bond that words couldn't quite capture.

He wasn't the kind of father who lectured or judged. He loved me the best way he knew how—with laughter, affection, and a spirit that refused to let life dim his light. That kind of love, though imperfect, became a compass for me.

The Man Beyond the Myths

It wasn't until I got older that I began to learn more about who my father really was. His family and friends told me stories—some hard to hear—about his struggles with addiction. They said he was a drug addict. But that wasn't the man I saw.

He never used drugs around me. He never let that world touch my world. To me, he was Daddy—the man who laughed loud, loved deeply, and gave joy without asking for anything in return. Looking back, I can see the red flags now—the moments that didn't quite add up—but I chose not to see them then. I chose love. I chose him.

Maybe that's what daughters do—we see the best in our fathers even when the world tells us to see the worst.

His struggle became my strength. Because of what he battled, my siblings and I made a silent vow: we would live differently. We would live free. None of us have ever turned to drugs. In his pain, we found our purpose.

Lessons from His Laughter

My father taught me more about living than anyone else. Not through advice or example, but through his energy—his insistence on joy even when life was hard. He showed me that laughter could be medicine, that love could exist even in broken places, and that strength didn't always have to look perfect.

He used to make the world brighter for everyone around him, and that light still lingers. Even now, at forty-nine, I carry it with me. His laughter echoes in my heart, a reminder that love, no matter how flawed, leaves something eternal behind.

He taught me that *living your life* means embracing every moment— both the joy and the pain—as opportunities to grow, learn, and connect. It means choosing to be present, to pursue passion, to live fully and freely. Daddy showed me that life is not about perfection—it's about presence.

The Steady Shore

When I think of my father now, I picture him standing at the edge of a storm—steady, unshaken, smiling through the wind. He was not perfect—no, far from it—but he was my steady shore in a restless sea. His laughter cracked through my darkest days. His love, flawed but real, became my foundation.

Because he was my dad, his impact lives deep within me—a quiet song of strength, joy, and grace.

Rest easy, Daddy.

Your laughter still echoes in my heart and your love will always accompany me.

Present, But Not Really There
Sasha Robinson

My name is Sasha Robinson. I'm 40 years old, and my father, Thomas Robinson, lives with me now. But if you think that means we've finally found closeness, or healing, or even peace, you'd be mistaken. His presence in my home now doesn't erase his absence from my life then. If anything, it's reopened wounds I never fully tended to.

Growing up, my father lived with us, but emotionally, I lived without him. He was physically there, yet not really *present*. I remember knowing he was in the house, but not in *my* life. He ran the streets, tangled up in his own issues. He was a veteran with mental health challenges, but that never translated to compassion or connection with me. We barely spoke. There was no father-daughter bonding, no "daddy's girl" moments, no safety net to catch me when life felt too big.

Silent Spaces and Missed Opportunities

When I look back on my childhood, the silence between us speaks louder than any argument we could have had. There were no real conversations. No advice. No protection. Just distance. And when he finally started showing up more…after a stroke left him weakened and dependent…it felt like life was playing a cruel joke on me. Now, I'm the caretaker. The daughter stepping up to care for the man who never made time for her.

I do it because I'm human. I do it because my mother passed away in June, and someone had to take him in. But caring for someone who didn't care for you? That's a different kind of grief.

How His Absence Shaped Me

There's no doubt that my father's emotional abandonment had a lasting impact. I found myself looking for the love I didn't get from him in other men. That empty space he left became a void I tried to fill; with attention, with relationships, with all the wrong things. I got pregnant at 17, and I remember the look on his face—disappointed. But how could he judge me when he had never been present to guide me?

I take responsibility for my choices. I won't blame him for everything. But I won't lie and pretend his absence didn't leave cracks in my foundation. He should have been there. Period.

The Weight of Now

Living with him now, I try to balance duty with distance. I make sure he's fed, safe, cared for—but that's it. We're not suddenly close. If anything, I still feel like the little girl watching her father walk past her as if she's invisible.

And yet… I'm not angry all the time. Just tired. Tired of pretending it didn't matter. Tired of carrying the emotional cost of his choices. Tired of waiting for an apology I know will never come.

Owning My Story

I consider myself a *Fatherless Daughter*. Not because he wasn't under the same roof—but because I still had to raise myself emotionally. I had to learn what it meant to be a woman without his guidance, learn what love should look like by trial and painful error. And now, even in the role of caregiver, I'm still learning how to care for someone without losing the parts of me he never nurtured in the first place.

This isn't a story with a neat ending. But it's *mine*. And I tell it not for sympathy, but for truth.

Surface-Level Love, Deep-Level Healing
Ashley Taylor

My name is Ashley Taylor. I'm 21 years old. On paper, I wasn't fatherless. Wayne Taylor, my dad, was around. Physically. But presence isn't the same thing as connection—and emotionally, he was distant. Still is.

Growing up, he was the kind of man who did only what was "needed." He asked how you were doing here and there, but never really sat down to talk. No daddy-daughter dates. No long conversations. No depth. If anything, he was more present with his video games than with me.

And while I love him, I resented him too—because my mother carried the weight of our world alone.

Growing Up Too Fast

I didn't get to be a carefree kid. As the oldest, I watched my mom drown in responsibilities—paying bills, helping with homework, holding it all together. And while my dad lived in the same house, I kept asking myself: *Why won't he help her?* Why did *I* have to be the one stepping in at 12 years old?

That frustration stayed with me. And it shaped how I saw love.

Looking for What I Didn't Get

My relationship with my dad made me crave love and protection in other places—especially from boys. In high school, I started using sex as a way to feel wanted, to feel seen. I convinced myself it meant someone cared. But the truth was, I didn't love myself enough to realize I deserved more than momentary affection. I didn't understand that my worth didn't come from being desired— but from being *whole*.

I became a master at hiding. On the surface, everyone loves me. I'm that girl—friendly, social, fun. But deep down? I felt lonely. Like no one *really* knew me. I kept everything bottled in, afraid to let people see the parts of me that were still hurting, still healing.

Wishing Things Were Different

I don't hate my father. I never have. But I do wish he had helped more. I wish he showed us, showed *me*, that we mattered beyond just the basics. I wish he had shown up for my mom—not just financially, but emotionally. That kind of absence made me grow up too quickly and left holes I tried to fill with the wrong things.

Learning to Love Me

Now, I'm learning what real healing looks like. I'm starting to understand that I can't rely on other people—especially not men— to make me feel loved or safe. That has to come from within. I'm learning to open up, to be vulnerable, to truly connect without fear or shame.

This chapter of my life isn't about blaming anyone. It's about recognizing the patterns, the pain, and deciding *not* to carry them forward. I'm writing a new story—one where I'm no longer just surviving off surface-level love, but building something deeper. With myself first.

Because I finally realize: I don't have to earn love through pain. I already deserve it.

The Soldier Who Stayed and Strayed
Anonymous

The Space Between

There are fathers who stay steady, whose love is simple and sure. And then there are fathers whose love feels like pieces— sometimes present, sometimes absent, sometimes hard to hold.

When your father is a soldier, you learn early that his world is divided: part family, part duty, part freedom. You learn that he can be both strong and distant, affectionate and detached, present and yet unreachable.

That was my father. And this is my story.

Growing Up With a Soldier

My father was a dedicated soldier. His uniform was pressed, his posture straight, his duty to his country clear. But when it came to family, when it came to intimacy, consistency wasn't always part of his story.

He was married multiple times, moving in and out of relationships that never seemed to hold. It wasn't that he didn't have emotions— he did. He could show affection, even tenderness—but not constantly. It was like he had compartments inside himself. One part of him knew how to be a provider, another part longed for freedom, and another part drifted in and out of connection.

As his daughter, I watched this pattern quietly. Sometimes I felt his presence. Other times, he was a shadow passing through. His love was there, but it was unpredictable.

Love in Pieces

I learned early that how my father treated women depended on where he was in life. When he lived in Mississippi, he seemed more rooted, more connected to family. His wife mattered then, because his world was grounded in the familiarity of kin.

But when he joined the Army, something shifted. The discipline of the military gave him strength and structure, but it also gave him freedom to be away—to step outside the rules of home. Distance became an open door to cheating, to straying, to detaching from the very women who wanted his heart.

I think, in truth, he always needed a woman. But he didn't always cherish the relationship. That reality has left an imprint on me.

His Impact on Me

Even now, I see how my father's choices echo into my own. How he treated women—how he both wanted them and failed to hold them—has shaped what I expect, what I fear, and what I long for.

It determines how I want to be treated by men. I crave consistency. I crave being cherished. But sometimes, I settle for being "needed," because that's what I saw him do. He needed women for companionship, for comfort, for stability—but didn't always honor them. And in some ways, I've fallen into that same cycle.

My Own Choices

I married a man for security. Not for love that burns bright, but for the safety of knowing someone was there. When that marriage ended in divorce, I thought I would break the pattern. But I didn't. I found myself spiraling into new relationships, again and again, for the same reason—security. Sometimes it was financial. Sometimes it was emotional. But always, it was about not being alone.

Because for me, being alone is terrifying. And when I look at it honestly, I wonder if I am more like my father than I ever wanted to admit.

The Reflection

My father wasn't absent. He wasn't abusive. He wasn't heartless. But he was complicated. And loving a complicated man leaves you with complicated lessons.

I am still learning what love should look like. Still learning how to demand not just presence, but cherishing. Still learning how to break patterns that feel inherited, even if they aren't inevitable.

And so, in my story, my father is both my teacher and my mirror. I see in him what I want to embrace—and what I must choose to let go.

Daddy's Girl, Daddy's Ghost
Anonymous

To the world, he was Ernest.
To me, he was everything I admired—and everything I feared
becoming.

My father was a walking contradiction: brilliant, dangerous, magnetic.
He was the kind of man who could fix anything, charm anyone, and
leave a trail of devastation behind him. He spoke multiple languages,
smelled like expensive cologne, drove a white Cadillac with red interior,
and dressed like he was headed to a jazz club in Harlem—even if he
was just running errands.

He was a king in his world. And his fists ruled it.

The Gift-Giver with a Heavy Hand

My earliest memories come wrapped in a paradox. My father gave the
best gifts—coats, toys, jewelry. But I quickly learned that gifts were his
way of apologizing for what came before. My mother would be
bruised, broken, silent—and then the shopping bags would appear.
Beautiful distractions. Temporary peace offerings.

I learned early: gifts weren't love. Gifts were guilt. And love, as I
saw it then, hurt more than it healed.

That lesson stayed with me. Now, as a 40-something-year-old
woman, I don't like to be spoiled. I don't trust it. A man brings me
flowers, and I wonder what he's done. A man asks where I am, and
I brace myself—not because he's wrong, but because control dressed
itself in care in my childhood home.

The Juke Joint Princess

After my parents divorced, I still spent my summers and holidays with
Daddy. He stopped drinking. He mellowed out. He was older, softer,
slower. During middle school, I even moved in with him.
That version of my father—sixty, stylish, easygoing—took me
everywhere. I was the only little girl in juke joints, bootleg houses, and
grown-folk spaces no child had business being in. But I didn't mind. I
loved being his shadow.

And I loved *him*—even if I feared what he was capable of. Even if I
watched what he did to my mother and wondered what parts of
that violence lived in me.

The Man I'm Still Looking For

I am, in so many ways, my father's daughter. Intelligent. Charismatic.
Generous. I want a partner who mirrors all his best qualities—minus the
harm. But I can't seem to find him. Maybe
that's because I've learned to be so guarded, I shut down men who
come too close.

A man asks too many questions, and I think he's trying to control me.
A man gives too many gifts, and I feel suffocated. My father's legacy
left me constantly measuring love against pain—trying to sort out
what's real and what's dangerous.

Becoming the Best of Him

I don't tolerate even a hint of control in my relationships. I'm fierce,
independent, and protective of my peace. And in that way, I've
become the *opposite* of my father.

But I'm also so much like him. I'm sharp. I know how to move through a room, how to make people feel something. I'm generous, magnetic, and unafraid to stand out.

The truth is, I've spent a lifetime trying to separate the man he was from the father he became—and trying to piece together the woman I want to be, somewhere in between.

I loved my father deeply. I still do. I just wish I didn't have to unravel him to understand myself.

Between Two Names: A Daughter's Journey Toward Peace
Laura Irvin

My name is Laura Irvin, and my story is threaded between two father figures: Jeff Roscoe, my biological father, and Theotis Herron, my stepfather. Their presence—or absence—has shaped me in ways I only began to understand in adulthood.

At 47, I carry both men's legacies in my memory. One man gave me life; the other helped shape it. Yet, even with two names, I often felt like a daughter suspended in-between identities, searching for something whole in a story that always felt partial.

A Fragmented Beginning

I was raised primarily by my mother and stepfather. Theotis married my mom when I was four, and from that point on, he assumed the role of my father. But there was always a space between us— something invisible but real. I never gave him the opportunity to truly be the father he might have wanted to be. Perhaps it was because I knew deep down he wasn't my biological father. Or perhaps, it was because I hadn't healed from the emotional absence of the one who was.

My biological father, Jeff, was largely a mystery to me throughout my childhood. I knew he was alive, but he was a distant shadow— an alcoholic, emotionally absent, and seemingly uninterested in knowing his daughter. For years, he was nothing more than a name. He didn't raise me. He didn't call. He didn't try. And in that void, I became what many would call a *Fatherless Daughter*.

It wasn't until I was in my mid-thirties that I truly "met" Jeff. By then, he was a paraplegic living in Maryland with his sister. She reached out and reconnected us through phone calls. He couldn't speak—he could only listen. And that made the process even harder. How do you rebuild something that never existed in the first place, especially when only one person can talk? I felt hurt. I felt abandoned. And still, I tried.

A Complex Home

Growing up, my relationship with Theotis was complicated. He was there—physically present, emotionally distant. He provided stability and took on the responsibility of being a father to me and my siblings. But love, at least the kind I yearned for, didn't come easily. My mom loved him, but their relationship was tumultuous. They drank heavily and fought often. I would hide in my brother's room during those nights, clinging to him while chaos brewed just outside the door.

Despite everything, Theotis remained. He stayed even when it was hard. There were periods of peace—especially after my mother went through detox and maintained sobriety for several years. But by the time my youngest sister graduated high school, their marriage had run its course. They divorced, and that chapter, too, closed quietly.

Even now, our relationship remains distant—not hostile, just muted. I love and respect Theotis for stepping in. But that deep, blood-born connection never quite formed. Maybe it couldn't. Maybe it wasn't meant to.

What It Meant to Be Fatherless

I consider myself a *Fatherless Daughter*. Not because there was never a man around—but because neither man could fully offer what I needed: security, love, consistency, belonging. I felt fatherless when Jeff left and never came back. I felt fatherless when Theotis showed up but remained just beyond reach.

I became fatherless not at birth, but over time—somewhere between ages 5 and 14, when I realized that the support I longed for would not come in the way I had hoped.

And yet, I survived. I grew. I married. I built a life. My stepfather, though not perfect, was encouraging. Stern but steady. He did what he could. And for that, I am grateful.

The Lingering Impact

My relationship with both men continues to affect my life in small and large ways. It influences how I trust others, how I parent, and how I define love. There's a resilience that grew out of that early emotional gap, but also a longing that never fully goes away.

I've learned to hold both truths at once: gratitude and grief. Respect and disappointment. Love and longing.

Final Reflections

Jeff remains more of a memory than a person. I didn't get to know him until it was too late. Theotis, though flawed, stood in the gap. And me—I continue the journey. A daughter between two names, finding peace with both.

Between Visits and Voices

Catherine Bass

I was born into a silence I never chose.

The kind that doesn't yell or scream.

The kind that lingers.

My name is Catherine Bass, and I am 21 years old.

I have no stories to pass on, no memories to revisit. Just a space where something—or someone—should be.

People ask sometimes. They assume. "What's your dad like?"

I've mastered the art of the half-smile and the quiet shrug.

They don't know that behind that silence, there's an ache I can't always explain. I am one of the girls who has grown up navigating life with a shadow where a man should have stood. A father who was never truly there. And yes, I consider myself a Fatherless Daughter.

My life has been shaped mostly by my mother; her presence, her voice, her strength. She's been my constant, and I love her for that. She's the one who's shown up, cheered me on, picked me up when I've fallen.

But even with all of her love, there has always been a missing piece. A quiet space where I imagine a father's advice should've been. His laughter. His protection. His words.

Instead, all I have is the echo of "what ifs" and "maybe somedays."

I know my father, but my relationship with him is complicated by the years he's spent behind bars.

When I was about five years old, my father was incarcerated. Since then, he has lived in a world separated from mine—behind walls and locked doors. Despite this, he has never completely disappeared from my life.

Though he's been physically absent, he's emotionally present in his own way. He calls me on the phone regularly, his voice carrying through the static, sometimes shaky but always full of love.

We visit each other too; in a room filled with cold rules, where words are exchanged but warm touches are impossible.

He is not the father who walks me to school or attends my events, but he is the father who, through these limited moments, shows me his care and effort. I see his dedication to our family in what little time we have, and I cherish it deeply.

Recently, I testified at my daddy's parole hearing; a moment I had both dreaded and prayed for. When the decision came back denied, it broke me in ways I can't describe. Five more years until the next chance. Five more years of waiting, of hoping, of believing that somehow things will be made right. I keep hearing that he doesn't even deserve to be there, and I hold on to that truth like air. My mom has always been honest. She's told me that he wasn't the best husband, but she's also made sure I knew he was an amazing father.

I remember him coming over every morning after the divorce just to get my brother and me ready for school. Even when life had shifted, he still showed up. He took us on family outings, made us laugh, and made sure we still felt whole.

Even now, he still shows up for me in ways that some dads on the outside don't. He gives advice over the phone, listens when I need him, and somehow still finds a way to be present, even from behind bars. So, I guess, in a way, I'm thankful that I at least have that. A father who loves me enough to show up however he can.

For a time, I also had a stepfather; a man who was present in my life and who I thought could fill some of the gaps left by my biological father. He lived in the same city, and for a while, it felt like maybe I wasn't so alone after all.

But when my mother and he divorced, everything changed. False promises never to be fulfilled.

He moved on with his life, remarried, and started a new family. He claims his new stepchildren as his own, but for me, he became a ghost in the background—someone who never calls, never visits, never checks in.

Living in the same city, yet feeling so distant, has been one of the hardest parts to understand. The man who once seemed like he might be a steady presence vanished from my world completely. It felt like being abandoned all over again… another father figure who chose someone else over me.

It's hard not to wonder why, and sometimes that silence hurts even more than his absence.

But I was never truly alone.

My grandfather stepped in and became a pillar of strength and love in my life. He is an amazing man and a powerful father figure who has shown me what unwavering support looks like. His steady presence has been a blessing. Proof that family can be found and built in unexpected ways.

And now, my story has taken a new turn.

Over the summer, my mom remarried to someone amazing, a man I now proudly call my "bonus dad."

For a while, I didn't want another father. I had learned to guard my heart, to protect that quiet space that had been left empty for so long. But he changed that gently, patiently, and on my time.

He gives me advice and takes care of me like his own, yet he's never pushed me or made any false promises. Instead, he's shown me through consistency, kindness, and respect what true fatherhood can look like.

In him, I've found a new kind of peace; a reminder that love doesn't always arrive when or how you expect it, but when it does, it can heal what's been broken.

Growing up, my mother has been my anchor, raising me with strength and love while navigating the challenges of my father's absence.

My father's incarceration has defined much of my childhood. It means learning to live between two worlds. The one outside, full of everyday life, and the one inside, where my father lives.

Even with the distance, I have never felt abandoned. His presence, though limited, reminds me that love can persist despite circumstances.

My relationship with my father has impacted me deeply. From him, I've learned resilience and patience. Lessons not always spoken, but lived.

His situation taught me that love isn't only about presence; it's about commitment, effort, and holding onto hope even when things seem impossible. I listen carefully to his voice on the phone and treasure our visits, because in those moments, I glimpse the man he is… the father who endures.

THE UNSPOKEN

"He heals the brokenhearted and binds up their wounds."
— *Psalm 147:3 (NIV)*

The Unspoken...

When the Father is the Storm

Not every father leaves.
 Some stay—and become the reason their daughters want to run.

They are in the pictures. At the dinner table. In the next room. Their names are on birth certificates and Christmas cards.
But presence does not always mean protection.

This section is for the daughters whose lives were shaped by fear long before they knew what to call it. For the women who flinched at kindness, not because they didn't want it—but because they were trained to believe it was always followed by something sharp.

These stories are not easy.
These pages hold truths that ache. That might trigger memories you've tried to forget. They speak of homes that looked normal from the outside—but inside, were battlegrounds of emotional manipulation, violence, neglect, control, or abuse. Not imagined. Not exaggerated. Just real, raw, and for too long—hidden.

Some fathers were storms in steel-toed boots.
Their rage filled the rooms before they did.
They didn't need to raise a hand—just a voice. A glare. A threat left hanging in the air like smoke.
Others were quieter, crueler in their indifference. Cold shoulders. Backhanded comments. Doors that closed and never opened again.
And for some daughters, the pain was even darker—unspeakable acts by the very man who was supposed to protect them from harm.

These are the daughters who learned to read moods like weather patterns. Who became experts in pretending. Who could sense danger from the way a key turned in a lock, or the shift in a man's breathing.

They hid their childhoods behind honor rolls, smiles in church pews, and silence.
Because how do you explain a kind of hurt that has no bruises?
How do you say "my dad is the reason I don't trust love" when everyone calls him a good man?

We do not tell these stories to shock you.

We tell them because they are still happening—in neighborhoods, in families, in people you know.
Because too many women grew up in houses where "discipline" was abuse, and "tough love" was just cruelty with better branding.
Because silence is the soil where generational pain takes root and grows.

But more than anything—
 We tell them because these women are still here.

Still breathing.
Still rebuilding.
Still refusing to be defined by the worst parts of their past.

This is not just a section about what was broken.
It's about what refused to stay broken.
About daughters who walked through fire and somehow came out
softer, not harder.
Wiser, not colder.
Fierce, but still capable of love.

So if you see yourself in these stories—if your father was the storm
instead of the shelter—know this:

You are not what he did.
You are not what he said.
You are not hard to love, or too much, or not enough.

You are worthy of peace.
You are capable of healing.
And you are absolutely not alone.

These pages belong to you, too.

And even if your story starts in darkness—
You still get to write the ending.

Breaking the Cycle, Becoming Whole
Anonymous

I'm 23 now, but in many ways, I feel older. Not because of age, but because of the work I've done to get here. My father, Jesse, wasn't the kind of man little girls dream about when they think of "daddy." He was abusive. I saw it. I lived it. I remember the fights, the pain he caused my mother, the way his words could cut even when he wasn't yelling.

But this isn't just a story of damage. It's one of clarity. One of healing.

For a long time, I didn't understand why I kept choosing the wrong men. Why I let myself be mistreated or believed love had to come with pain. But two years ago, I said enough. I entered a program called *Break The Cycles*, and it changed everything. I committed myself to a full year of self-growth, of deep internal work, and it was there I learned that the root of so many of my wounds traced back to him.

To my father.

Seeing the Truth Without the Hate

He wasn't always terrible. That's the complicated part. He could be kind, even fun. He worked hard and provided for us. But his decisions; his infidelity, his manipulation, his violence, cast a long shadow. I carried that shadow into every relationship, into the way I saw men, the way I saw myself.

But healing doesn't mean rewriting the past to make it prettier. It means telling the truth, and still choosing to move forward. My truth is this: My father did not know how to love me the way I needed. But I believe he didn't know how to be a father because he never had a real one himself. And that, I no longer hold against him.

Choosing Differently

Today, I'm grateful. Not for the pain, but for the awareness. If I hadn't faced it, I might still be chasing broken men trying to fix something in them, or in me. But now, I know better. I know I am worthy of love that doesn't hurt. I know I don't have to settle for someone who reminds me of my father's worst traits.

I'm no longer filling voids. I'm learning to be whole on my own.

This Is Closure

I share this not out of anger, but out of freedom. There's power in telling your story, especially when it no longer controls you. My father's choices shaped parts of me, yes. But now, *my choices* are shaping the woman I'm becoming.

I am not my past.
I am not his pain.
I am not a Fatherless Daughter forever—
I am a healed one.

Shadows in the Silence
Anonymous

I don't use my real name here. Not because I'm ashamed, but because some wounds are too raw to expose in daylight. I am just… Anonymous.

My father? He was the kind of man who taught me fear before he taught me love. Not with words, but with silence and storm. When I think of him, I don't see a father, I see a shadow that follows me everywhere, dark and cold, sometimes lurking, sometimes striking without warning.

He wasn't the man who held me when I cried. He wasn't the voice that whispered "I love you" or the arms that made the world safe. Instead, he was the loud bursts of anger at nothing, the slammed doors, the nights I tiptoed around the house, hoping not to wake the beast.

He was there… but not really. Living under the same roof but never truly present. He drank too much, disappeared too often, and when he was home, the house became a minefield. I learned early to stay small, to be quiet, to disappear into the corners.

I remember one Christmas when I was ten. Instead of presents and laughter, there were shattered dishes and shouting. My mother cried silently in the kitchen while I hid under the table, clutching my little sister close, promising her it would be okay, even when it wasn't.

As I grew older, the wounds deepened. His absence wasn't just physical. It was emotional neglect wrapped in anger and disappointment. He never came to my school events, never asked how I was doing, never offered advice or encouragement. The only thing I heard from him were criticisms sharp enough to cut deep.

I was his disappointment—his failure.

And I believed it. For years, I carried that weight. I thought if I were better, if I were different, maybe he would stay. Maybe he would love me.

But he never did.

He walked out when I was thirteen. Didn't say goodbye. Didn't look back. Left my mother and us to pick up the pieces of a broken family.

For a long time, I felt invisible, abandoned twice. Once by his presence, once by his absence.

I grew up angry, confused, broken. I struggled to trust men, to believe I was worthy of love. I chased approval in dangerous places, made choices that hurt me, because I didn't know how to love myself without his approval.

That pain followed me into adulthood. I married an abusive alcoholic who mirrored my father's cruelty. His words were knives; his hands, unpredictable storms. I stayed longer than I should have because I thought love meant sacrifice, that pain was a measure of devotion. Maybe if I could fix him, maybe if I stayed silent and small enough, I could finally earn the kind of love I never had.

It took years to break free. Years to hear my own voice over the noise of fear and shame. To realize that love should not hurt. That I deserved safety, kindness, respect.

But even now, the echoes linger. Sometimes I catch myself shrinking in fear or doubting my worth. Sometimes I wonder if I'll ever fully heal from the father who never held me and the husband who tried to break me.

Still, I am learning.

I still carry scars from him. The silence he left behind is deafening. But I'm filling that silence with my own voice, my own strength, my own story.

I am more than his failure. I am more than the shadow he cast.

I am a daughter... broken but healing, lost but finding my way, silent no longer.

The House with No Apologies
Anonymous

My father never hit me.

That's what I told myself for years, like it was some kind of prize. Like I had dodged the worst of it. Like verbal assault, emotional manipulation, and psychological warfare were easier to survive just because they didn't leave bruises.

But bruises fade.
The kind of damage he did? That settles into your bones. It rearranges your wiring. It teaches your body how to stay tense even when there's no threat because you learned to never relax.

He was the kind of man whose footsteps made the walls shiver. The kind whose silence was louder than shouting. The kind who could dismantle your whole sense of self with one look.

Some mornings, he was just quiet… indifferent. You'd pass him the salt at breakfast and he wouldn't look up. Some days, he'd slam doors just because he could. Other times, he'd rant for hours over nothing: the TV too loud, the shoes at the door, the way my mother breathed wrong. His anger was random, unpredictable, and always looking for a target.

He didn't use fists. His weapon was his mouth.

> "You're a burden."
> "You'll never be anything."
> "You're just like your mother—weak."
> "You're lucky I let you live here."

Sometimes I'd be halfway down the hall before I realized I was crying. The shame snuck up that fast. I learned to cry quietly. I learned to sit in my closet with the door shut and press my knees into my chest until the fear passed.

By nine, I was fluent in survival. I learned how to hold my breath and move without being noticed. How to read a room in five seconds flat. How to predict an explosion by the way his jaw clenched.

My mother tried to be soft in a house full of shards. She worked long hours and juggled bills and made excuses. But she stayed. Maybe out of fear. Maybe because she believed the same lie I did. That this was just what life was.

And that made it worse.

Because when your mother stays with the man who breaks you in pieces, it teaches you to normalize the breaking.

It taught me that love could be cruel.
 That being quiet kept you safe.
 That affection was something you earned by shrinking.

So I did what many daughters do: I looked for love that felt familiar.

At 22, I married a man just like my father. The resemblance wasn't just emotional, it was eerie. He had the same explosive temper, the same charismatic mask he wore in public, the same knack for twisting everything into my fault.

He told me what to wear. Who I could talk to. He cheated and lied and gaslit me until I questioned everything, especially my own worth. And when I cried, he said I was dramatic. When I got quiet, he called me cold.

I thought if I just loved him better, he'd change.
I thought I could rescue him.
But I was the one who needed saving.

The turning point came when I was standing in our dark kitchen, holding my newborn son to my chest. My husband was in the next room screaming, raging over dinner not being ready, throwing a chair against the wall so hard it cracked the plaster.

My son flinched in my arms. And
something in me shattered.

That night, I packed a bag, strapped my baby into his car seat, and drove away from everything I thought was love.

Leaving wasn't easy. It was court dates, therapy, nights I couldn't sleep because I was scared he'd show up. It was shame and grief and learning to live with the guilt of having ignored red flags.

But I left.

And that's when the healing began.

Even now, the damage lingers. I still flinch when someone raises their voice. I still question my worth on bad days. I still catch myself apologizing for simply existing. And the strangest, most painful part?

I still want my father to be proud of me.
The same man who tore me down. The one who never once said sorry.

He called it "discipline." Said he was just "raising me right." To him, emotions were weakness and compassion was a luxury we couldn't afford. But what he really taught me was how to ignore myself, how to become invisible, how to pretend everything was fine.

It wasn't love. It was control. It was fear.
And I carried that inheritance into my marriage like a wound I didn't know how to stop bleeding.

Now, I'm unlearning.

I'm rebuilding myself piece by piece with therapy, with faith, with boundaries that used to terrify me. I am parenting my son with tenderness I never knew. I am becoming the woman I needed as a child.

Some days, I still hear his voice in my head telling me I'm too much, or not enough. But that voice doesn't get to be the narrator anymore.

I do.

Because some fathers destroy.
But some daughters survive anyway. And
some daughters rise.

The Man in the Doorway
Anonymous

He never wore a mask, but somehow, I never knew who he really was. My father. The man in the doorway.

Not the doorway of comfort or protection. No, he stood in doorways with a belt in one hand and a bottle in the other. Always watching. Always judging. Always taking up space with his rage.

He didn't love us. At least not in any language we understood. His love was conditional. His love had rules. Be quiet. Be perfect. Be invisible when I'm angry. Be grateful when I'm not.

I remember once—just once—he took me to get ice cream. I was maybe six. I told everyone for months like it was a miracle. Like I'd just been handed the moon. That one scoop of strawberry was the only softness I ever got from him. Everything else was jagged edges and emotional bruises.

He called me names that still echo in my spine:
"Stupid girl."
"Fat like your mother."
"You'll never be anything."
And worse.

He didn't hit me often. But when he did, he made it count. Not just with his hands, but with the way he made me feel worthless afterward, like I had asked for it. Like I had ruined *his* day. Like I should apologize for bleeding.

He never apologized. Not once.

He cheated on my mother openly, shamelessly, and called it "a man's business." When she cried, he laughed. When she begged, he mocked. I watched her crumble in real time, shrinking a little more every year until she barely had a voice left.

I swore I would never be like her.
I swore I would never marry someone like him.

And then I did.

Different face. Same anger. Same lies. Same need to control.
At first, I thought I was choosing love, but really, I was just choosing familiarity. Trauma knows how to disguise itself as home.

My ex-husband never had to raise a hand. He could destroy me with a single look. He manipulated my mind until I questioned everything about myself—my worth, my memories, even my sanity.

I didn't leave for years. I told myself I could handle it. That I wasn't my mother. That I was stronger. But I wasn't stronger. I was scared.

It took therapy. It took faith. It took my children looking at me the way I used to look at my mother for me to say, "Enough."

And now, I look back at the man in the doorway.
Not with hate.
But not with forgiveness either.
Not yet.

He left a wreckage I am still sifting through.
I have learned that some fathers break more than homes; they break spirits.
They don't always leave bruises on the skin, but their fingerprints live inside your thoughts.
In the way you flinch when someone raises their voice.
In the way you apologize for taking up space.

But I am learning, slowly, that I am not the names he called me. I am not the shame he gave me.
I am not the daughter of his destruction… I am the survivor of it.

I used to ask, "Why did he stay if he hated us so much?"
Now I ask, "Why did I ever believe his hate was my fault?"

Some fathers should never be given the title.
And some daughters will rise anyway.
 I'm one of them.

Her Name Is Daughter

She is not just a statistic.

Not just a product of her father's absence or presence.

She is a story in motion—a woman shaped by what she had, what she didn't, what she lost, what she fought for, and what she became.

Over these pages, we've heard the voices of daughters whose fathers never knew their birthdays… and those who never missed one. We've sat in silence with girls who waited by the phone for a call that never came, and we've smiled with women who had their fathers walk them down the aisle with pride shining in their eyes.

We've met Catherine—a daughter born into silence, who knew her father only through glass walls and monitored calls. A girl who once held hope for a relationship and watched it dissolve when her stepfather remarried and claimed a new family across town. A girl whose heart has been broken more than once by men she called "Dad" — but who still holds tight to the strength of her mother and the unwavering presence of her grandfather. Her story reminds us that fatherlessness isn't always about physical absence. Sometimes, it's about being emotionally abandoned while fully in view.

We've seen the paradox: some daughters, despite good fathers who showed up day after day, still found themselves lost in the maze of toxic love. And others, left fatherless before they could even speak, somehow unearthed healing, self-worth, and healthy relationships in spite of all the odds stacked against them.

We've peeled back the labels—the casual, dismissive "Daddy Issues,"
the clinical "Father Complex"—and laid bare the raw,
aching truth beneath. Because there is nothing small about the ache of
not being seen. Nothing funny about searching for love where it
simply doesn't live. Nothing simple about forgiving a man who
couldn't or wouldn't be what he should have been.

And yet… so many daughters rise.

They rise from silence to song.
 From abandonment to affirmation.
 From wounds to wisdom.

They write new endings to old stories. They
build homes with love, not with scars. They
break generational cycles of pain.
They become the parents they always wished for—or the exact
opposite, reclaiming their power in their own way.

Because being a daughter is never just about biology.
 It's about longing and learning.
 Loss and discovery.
 It's about choosing—every single day—to grow.

To the woman still grieving. To
the woman still healing.
To the woman who wonders if she was ever enough.

You were.
You are.
You always have been.

This may be the last chapter of this book, but it is only the beginning of your story.

Whether you are defined by his presence or his absence, whether you carry deep scars or are still searching for answers—your voice matters.

Your story matters.

You matter.

And now it's your turn.

Speak your truth.
Write your story.
Heal your heart.

Reach out to others who walk this path.
Build communities that lift and listen.
Refuse to let silence be the legacy.

Whether you whisper your pain in secret or shout your triumph to the world, know this: you hold the power to reclaim your narrative.

You can still say the words that so many daughters have held quietly inside, afraid to speak, afraid to need:

"Just call me Daddy's girl."

Or… simply,

"Just call me Daughter."

Because in the end, that's who you are—always and forever.

Epilogue
Beyond the Pages

The stories you have read are more than chapters in a book, they are echoes of lives lived, wounds tended, and hearts mended. They remind us that the father-daughter relationship is not a simple blueprint but a complex mosaic, full of shadows and light.

If you are reading this and feel the weight of absence or the sting of broken promises, know this: your journey is not a solitary one. Many have walked this path before you, carrying their pain and hope in equal measure.

Healing is not linear. It's messy, unpredictable, and deeply personal. Some days, it will feel like a whisper of peace. Other days, a storm of grief. Both are okay. Both are part of becoming whole.

To those daughters whose fathers were present in body but absent in heart, you are not invisible. Your pain is valid, and your strength is fierce.

To those who grew up with loving fathers but still struggle with love and trust... you are seen. Your questions are real, and your courage to keep searching is a victory.

To the fathers who try and stumble, who love imperfectly but earnestly... thank you. Keep showing up. Keep listening. Keep learning.

And to every woman who picks up this book, whether to see herself reflected or to understand another's story, you are part of a larger conversation. A movement toward healing, compassion, and understanding.

May you find peace in your own story, whatever it looks like. May you find the love you deserve in yourself and others.

And may you always remember: The relationship you have with your father may have shaped you, but it does not define the fullness of who you are.

You are more than a daughter.
You are a force.
You are enough.

Thank you for walking this path with us.

Resource Guide
Finding Strength, Healing, and Support

Whether you grew up with an absent father, a challenging father, or even a loving father but still carry wounds, healing is possible. You are not alone on this journey. Here are some trusted resources to help you find support, community, and tools to reclaim your story:

Therapy and Counselling

- **Individual Therapy:** A safe place to explore your feelings about your father, process trauma, and build self-worth. Look for therapists specializing in family dynamics, trauma, or attachment issues.

- **Group Therapy:** Connecting with other daughters who share similar experiences can provide comfort and validation.

- **Online Therapy Options:** Services like BetterHelp, Talkspace, and Open Path offer affordable and accessible mental health support.

Books and Memoirs

- *"The Secret Life of Fathers: An Unexpected Guide to Understanding MEN... and Fathers"* — The Father-Daughter Project

- *"Raising Boys by Design"* by Gregory L. Jantz, PhD — Offers a practical blueprint to help you build a HERO—one who values Honor, Enterprise, Responsibility, and Originality.

- *"The Absent Father Effect"* by Susan E. Swartz — Investigates the impact of absent – physically or emotionally – and inadequate fathers on the lives and psyches of their daughters

- *"Healing the Father Wound"* by H. Norman Wright — Words of caring and restoration for women whose dads were missing from their lives--whether emotionally, physically, or spiritually

Support Communities and Forums

- **Online Support Groups:** Facebook groups like *Daughters of Absent Fathers* or *Fatherless Daughters Healing* offer safe spaces for sharing and encouragement.

- **Nonprofit Organizations:** Groups such as *National Fatherhood Initiative* and *The Fatherhood Project* provide resources and workshops focused on family healing.

- **Local Community Centers:** Many cities offer free or low-cost support groups for family and relationship issues—check community boards or health centers.

Healing Through Creativity

- **Journaling:** Write letters to your father—whether sent or unsent—to express feelings and gain clarity.

- **Art Therapy:** Drawing, painting, or crafting can help process emotions beyond words.

- **Writing Groups:** Joining a creative writing or memoir group can help you shape your story and find your voice.

Building Healthy Relationships

- **Books on Relationship Skills:** Titles like *"Attached"* by Amir Levine and Rachel Heller offer insight into attachment styles and relationship patterns.

- **Workshops on Boundaries and Self-Worth:** Learning how to set healthy boundaries is key to breaking cycles and forming fulfilling connections.

- **Mentorship Programs:** Seek mentors—especially women who have navigated similar challenges—to provide guidance and example.

For Fathers and Families

- **Parenting Classes:** To support fathers who want to reconnect or improve their relationships.

- **Family Therapy:** When safe and appropriate, family counseling can open dialogue and healing.

Emergency and Crisis Support

- **National Domestic Violence Hotline:** 1-800-799-7233

- **Crisis Text Line:** Text HOME to 741741

- **Suicide Prevention Lifeline:** 988

Final Thought

Your journey is unique, and healing isn't linear. Take one step at a time. Reach out when you're ready. And remember: no matter your past, your future holds possibility. You deserve peace, love, and joy.

If you're reading this, you've already begun.

Keep going.

Appendix

Survey

Informed Consent

Title: *Just Call Me Daddy: The Impact of the Father-Daughter Relationship*

You are invited to participate in a research study. The purpose of the study is to look at relationships between daughters and fathers, explore the understanding of being fathered or fatherless, and the impact these relationships may or may not have had on your life thus far.

Procedures:
If you decide to participate, you will complete a one-time survey on a secure website. Your responses will remain confidential.

Risks:
Participation may cause emotional upset. If so, contact the primary researcher, **Dr. Shanta McClurkin Joyner**.

Benefits:
You may gain personal insight about your relationship with your father.

Voluntary Participation and Withdrawal:
Participation is voluntary. You may withdraw at any time without penalty.

Confidentiality:
All information will be kept confidential.

Contact:
Dr. Shanta McClurkin Joyner

Survey Questions & Answer Choices

Email
(Short answer)

Participation*

- I agree to participate in this survey.

- I no longer wish to participate in this study.

Release Form*

- I have submitted the author release form to Dr. Shanta McClurkin Joyner.

- I have NOT submitted the author release form to Dr. Shanta McClurkin Joyner.

- I no longer wish to participate in this study.

Do you choose to be anonymous, use a pseudo name, or use your real name?

- Anonymous (author selects a fictitious name)

- Pseudo Name (you provide a fictitious name)

- Real Name

If you chose pseudo name or real name, please type it as it should appear in the publication.
(Short answer)

How would you like your father's name to appear? Please type it below.
(Short answer)

What is your current age?
(Short answer)

Who raised you?

- Mother and father

- Mother and step-father

- Mother and her partner/significant other

- Adoptive parents

- Mother

- Aunt

- Aunt and uncle

- Grandmother

- Grandmother and grandfather

- Father

- Father and step-mother

- Father and his partner/significant other

- Uncle

- Grandfather

- Older sibling

- Foster family

- Other: *(Short answer)*

How would you describe your racial/ethnic background?

- American Indian or Alaskan Native

- African American/Black

- White

- Hispanic or Latina

- Asian

- Native Hawaiian or Pacific Islander

Which of the following best describes your current relationship status?

- Married

- Widowed

- Divorced

- Separated

- In a domestic partnership or civil union

- Single, but cohabiting with a significant other

- Single, never married

How would you describe your relationship as a child with your father?

- Extremely close

- Very close

- Somewhat close

- Not very close

- Detached

- Very detached

- Extremely detached

- I never saw my father

- My father was deceased

- Other: *(Short answer)*

How would you identify the status of your parents' relationship when you were growing up? (Select all that apply.)

- Happily married

- Somewhat happily married

- Unhappily married

- Very unhappily married

- Abusive

- Separated

- Divorced

- Never married

- Never met my father

- My father was deceased

How would you describe your father's emotional presence in your life during your adolescence?

- Emotionally present

- Somewhat emotionally present

- Somewhat emotionally absent

- Completely emotionally absent

- I never saw my father

- My father was deceased

How would you describe your father's physical presence in your home during adolescence?

- Living at home

- Living in and out of our home

- Living away from our home

- Incarcerated

- Overseas

- I do not know where my father was

- My father was deceased

How would you describe your relationship with your father now that you are an adult?

- Very close

- Somewhat close

- Somewhat distant

- Very distant

- Estranged

- My father is deceased

- I don't know my father

- I am still an adolescent

Check all circumstances below that you CONSIDER might define a Fatherless Daughter:

- Father is deceased

- Parents are separated or divorced and the father is rarely or never around

- Father has deserted the family

- Father is abusive

- Father is emotionally absent

- Father is an addict

- Father is living overseas

- Father gave daughter up for adoption

- Father is incarcerated

- Father has had a long-term illness, which has mentally debilitated him

Do you consider yourself a Fatherless Daughter?

- Yes

- No

- Maybe

- I was a Fatherless Daughter once but am now reconnected with him

If you consider yourself a Fatherless Daughter, please identify the age that you became Fatherless.

- Birth

- 0–4

- 5–9

- 10–14

- 15–19

- 20–24

- 25–29

- 30–39

- 40–49

- 50 years or older

- I am not Fatherless

Select all of the responses that are true for you:

- I never met my father

- My father gave me up for adoption

- My father passed away

- My father deserted the family

- My parents got separated or divorced

- My father was abusive

- My father was an addict

- My father was incarcerated

- My father lived overseas

- Other: *(Short answer)*

Describe what you know about your father.
(Paragraph response)

Do you think your relationship with your father has an impact on your life now?

- Yes

- No

- Maybe

If yes, how?
(Paragraph response)

Share whatever you would like to share about your father here:
(Paragraph response)

Share whatever you would like to share about your life decisions here:
(Paragraph response)

Acknowledgments

First and foremost, I give all glory and honor to God, the ultimate Father, whose love has guided me, sustained me, and given me the words to bring this vision to life.

To my father, Jesse James McClurkin, Jr., thank you for being the blueprint. Your love, patience, and strength are the heartbeat of this book.

To my mother, Dianne Harts McClurkin, your grace, strength, and unwavering love have shaped me into the woman I am today. Thank you for being my constant example of quiet power and resilience.

To my husband, James Joyner, IV (Jimmy), thank you for being my peace, my partner, and my green flag. You have shown me that love can be soft, steady, and safe… a home I never want to leave.

To my children, Catherine and Marcus, you are my greatest joy and my proudest purpose. Watching you grow reminds me daily why love and legacy matter so deeply.

To my sister, Jessica McClurkin Gates, thank you for being my lifelong friend, encourager, and truth-teller. Your love and laughter have carried me through so many seasons.

To the women who bravely shared their stories, your honesty and vulnerability gave this book its soul. I am honored that you trusted me with your truths. One of you is no longer with us, but your voice still echoes through these pages. This book carries your light. To my family, friends, and village, thank you for your encouragement, your prayers, and your constant belief in me. You reminded me that this book wasn't just mine to write; it was mine to finish.

And finally, to every daughter reading this book — may you find healing, clarity, and hope within these pages. Whether your father was your hero or your heartbreak, may you learn that your story still has beauty, and your love still has purpose.
With gratitude and grace,
Dr. Shanta McClurkin Joyner— A Blessed Daughter

About the Author

Dr. Shanta McClurkin Joyner is an accomplished educator, leader, and advocate who believes in the power of love, learning, and legacy. A native of South Carolina and now residing in Columbus, Georgia, she has devoted her life to empowering others through education, the arts, and community service.

Dr. Joyner holds multiple degrees from Columbus State University, including a Doctorate in Curriculum and Leadership. As an academic coach, college instructor and adjunct professor, she has inspired countless students and educators to rise to their highest potential. She also is a licensed REALTOR, another service-oriented career. Her leadership is rooted in compassion, excellence, and faith; qualities she brings into every classroom, every conversation, and every community she serves.

Beyond her professional career, Dr. Joyner is a passionate advocate for women and girls. She works to uplift those struggling with self-esteem, identity, and healing from the effects of broken or complicated father–daughter relationships. Through her writing, mentoring, and outreach, she encourages others to rebuild their confidence, reclaim their voices, and redefine what love and strength look like.

Her community impact extends through initiatives like the *Dr. Shanta McClurkin Joyner Creative Writing Contest*, which celebrates young writers in grades K–12, and the *Shanta & Jimmy Joyner Community Spirit Award*, which honors compassionate, creative, and service-driven 5th-grade students. She also celebrates unity and empowerment through the arts, believing that creativity is a healing language of its own.

In recognition of her dedication to education, leadership, and service, Dr. Joyner has received the *Presidential Lifetime Achievement Award*, one of the nation's highest honors for volunteerism and community impact. She is also a proud member of Alpha Kappa Alpha Sorority, Incorporated, where she continues her lifelong commitment to sisterhood and service to all mankind.

Dr. Joyner's inspiration for *Just Call Me Daddy: The Impact of the Father–Daughter Relationship* began as a personal search for understanding. After years of reflection and research, she turned her experiences, and the voices of many other women, into a narrative that speaks to both pain and purpose. Her father, Jesse James McClurkin, Jr., continues to be the foundation of her work and her faith in the enduring bond between fathers and daughters. She now shares her life with her husband, Jimmy Joyner, and their children, continuing to live out the very lessons of love, grace, and leadership that fill the pages of her book.

Through her story and her service, Dr. Shanta McClurkin Joyner embodies what it means to turn purpose into power — to become the standard, not the statistic.

www.ingramcontent.com/pod-product-compliance
Lightning Source LLC
Chambersburg PA
CBHW032138040426
42449CB00005B/297